BOOKS BY ANTHONY HECHT

POETRY

Flight Among the Tombs   1996
The Transparent Man   1990
Collected Earlier Poems   1990
The Venetian Vespers   1979
Millions of Strange Shadows   1977
The Hard Hours   1967
A Summoning of Stones   1954

TRANSLATION

Aeschylus's Seven Against Thebes   1975
(WITH HELEN BACON)

ESSAYS AND CRITICISM

On the Laws of the Poetic Art   1995
(ANDREW W. MELLON LECTURES IN THE FINE ARTS)
The Hidden Law: the Poetry of W. H. Auden   1993
Obbligati   1986

EDITOR

Jiggery-Pokery: A Compendium of Double Dactyls   1967
(WITH JOHN HOLLANDER)
The Essential George Herbert   1987

FLIGHT AMONG THE TOMBS

WOOD ENGRAVINGS BY
LEONARD BASKIN

FLIGHT AMONG THE TOMBS

POEMS BY

ANTHONY HECHT

Alfred A. Knopf   *New York*   1996

THIS IS A BORZOI BOOK
PUBLISHED BY ALFRED A. KNOPF, INC.

http://www.randomhouse.com/

ACKNOWLEDGMENTS: *The Presumptions of Death* was published in a limited edition of sixty copies by the Gehenna Press, Rockport, Maine, 1995.

Death the Judge: *The New Yorker*
Prospects: *The New Yorker*
The Mysteries of Caesar: *The New Yorker*
A Death in Winter: *The New Yorker*
Death the Inquisitor: *Sewanee Theological Review*
Death the Poet: *Sewanee Review*
Death the Whore: *Yale Review*
Death the Film Director: *Baylor University*
The Whirligig of Time: *Janus*
A Ruminant: *Southern Review*
Matisse: Blue Interior with Two Girls: *Colorado Review*
Proust on Skates: *The New Republic*
The Life of Crime: *Press*
To Fortuna Parvulorum: *Paris Review*
Là-Bas: A Trance: *Paris Review*
Death Sauntering About: *Poetry*
Death the Mexican Revolutionary: *Poetry*
Death the Punchinello: *Poetry*
Death the Archbishop: *Poetry*
Death the Painter: *Poetry*
Death the Copperplate Printer: *Poetry*
For James Merrill: An Adieu: *Poetry*

I should also like to express my gratitude to the Rockefeller Foundation and its Villa Serbelloni, where some of the poems in this collection were written.

Library of Congress Cataloging-in-Publication Data

Hecht, Anthony, 1923–
    Flight among the tombs : poems / by Anthony Hecht.–1st ed.
       p. cm.
    ISBN 0-679-45095-5
    I. Title.
PS3558.E28F58   1996
811'.54–dc20   96-19619
                                                              CIP

Manufactured in the United States of America
First Edition

For H E L E N *and* E V A N

Let Mattithiah bless with the Bat,
who inhabiteth the desolations of pride,
and flieth amongst the tombs.

CHRISTOPHER SMART

CONTENTS

I *The Presumptions of Death*

II *Proust on Skates*

Contents

I   THE PRESUMPTIONS OF DEATH

WOOD ENGRAVINGS BY LEONARD BASKIN

DEATH SAUNTERING ABOUT

The crowds have gathered here by the paddock gates
And racing silks like the flags of foreign states
    Billow and snap in the sun,
And thoroughbreds prance and paw the turf, the race
Is hotly contested, for win and show and place,
    Before it has yet begun.

The ladies' gowns in corals and mauves and reds,
Like fluently-changing variegated beds
    Of a wild informal garden,
Float hither and yon where gentlemen advance
Questions of form, the inscrutable ways of chance,
    As edges of shadow harden.

Among these holiday throngs, a passer-by,
Mute, unremarked, insouciant, saunter I,
    One who has placed—
Despite the tumult, the pounding of hooves, the sweat,
And the urgent importance of everybody's bet—
    No premium on haste.

DEATH THE HYPOCRITE

You claim to loathe me, yet everything you prize
Brings you within the reach of my embrace.
I see right through you though I have no eyes;
You fail to know me even face to face.

Your kiss, your car, cocktail and cigarette,
Your lecheries in fancy and in fact,
Unkindnesses you manage to forget,
Are ritual prologue to the final act

And certain curtain call. Nickels and dimes
Are but the cold coin of a realm that's mine.
I'm the acute accountant of your crimes
As of your real estate. Bristlecone pine,

Whose close-ringed chronicles mock your regimen
Of jogging, vitamins, and your strange desire
To disregard your assigned three-score and ten,
Yields to my absolute instrument of fire.

You know me, friend, as Faustus, Baudelaire,
Boredom, Self-Hatred, and, still more, Self-Love.
Hypocrite lecteur, mon semblable, mon frère,
Acknowledge me. I fit you like a glove.

DEATH DEMURE

I am retiring in more ways than one,
Quiet and noncommittal, a wallflower.
Reserving comment for some later hour,
I shall speak only "when all's said and done."

I hover secretly in the nightshade's
Nectar and dark, preparing my critique
Of life and manners. It's my turn to speak
When the last trump is played, in and with spades.

The softness of my voice inspires high hopes,
Weaving its way through alien environs,
Lovely as the cantatas of the Sirens
That made Odysseus heave against his ropes.

The original sheet-music of those *Femmes
Fatales* is mine, its vocal line expressive of
Sorrow? Frustration? A hopeless thirst for love?
"Nobody knows how dry (and shy) I am."

PEEKABOO

The longer thou livest, the more fool thou.

I

Go hide! Go hide! But through the latticework
    Of my upraised bone hands
I see athlete and statesman, priest and clerk
    Step forth as deodands,

Risking more than they know of life and limb
    In playing Peekaboo—
Whose happiest chances couldn't be called "slim"—
    I've tagged each: ICU

I I

Cry, baby, cry!
You've got two reasons why.
The first is being born at all;
The second, my peremptory call.
Cry, baby, cry!

Weep, baby, weep!
No solaces in sleep.
Nightmare will ruin your repose
And daylight resurrect your woes.
Weep, baby, weep!

I I I

Bah, bah, black sheep, you supply the needs
Plaguing mourners: stylish widows' weeds,
Haute couture for all the fashion shows.
Black is the color of my true love's clothes.

9

ALL OUT

This is the way we play our little game:
While I count up to ten, the others hide.
Do what you will, it always ends the same.

Some make a classical physique their aim
And, courting lust or envy, they decide
That is the way we play our little game.

Some seek the fragile garnitures of fame,
While some drop out, claiming, to salve their pride,
"Do what you will, it always ends the same."

Others attempt to put the world to shame,
Rejoicing when their flesh is mortified.
This is the way we play our little game

Of penance and contrition, meant to tame
A fear that we shall yet be caught and tried.
Do what you will, it always ends the same,

As careful studies of the odds proclaim,
And, although universally denied,
This *is* the way we play our little game.
Do what you will, it always ends the same.

DEATH RIDING INTO TOWN

Here comes Clint Eastwood riding into town,
      One of the horsey Four
Of the Apocalypse, who won renown
      With Famine, Plague and War.

Note the official badge he seems to flaunt,
      His casual offhand grace,
Ponder his polished six-guns and his gaunt
      Uncommonly pale face.

Dürer observed him pass at an easy trot,
      Accompanied by the Devil;
To some a hero by whom the human lot
      Is finally bulldozed level.

Exalted manna is his name and sweet
      To all the long suffering,
Who kneel to embrace him, clasping his bone feet,
      His scythe, ashes and sting,

While to the light of heart and proud of purse
      Encountered on his way
He smiles his cryptic smile and bids a terse
      "Go ahead, make my day!"

DEATH THE INQUISITOR

My testimonies are wonderful to the ears of the wise;
    They shall not be gainsaid by the ignorant.
Who has searched more deeply,
    Or reached a more perfect understanding?
I have ministered to the needs of maggots
    And confabulated with the least of ants.
In the tenements of the worm, in the mansions of the spider
    I have kept my counsel and watched.
I have conversed with the skulls of jackals
    And interpreted the long silences.
Observing the slow accretions of coral,
    I have rejoiced in perfect peace.
Who shall number the generations of the microbe,
    Or the engenderings of the common bacillus?
Who has attended the pathologies of the whelk,
    Or measured the breathing of the lungfish?
I abide the corruption of tungsten,
    The decay of massed granite.
I shall press to the core of every secret.
    There is no match for my patience.

DEATH THE OXFORD DON

Sole heir to a distinguished laureate,
I serve as guardian to his grand estate,
And grudgingly admit the unwashed herds
To the ten-point mausoleum of his words.
Acquiring over years the appetite
And feeding habits of a parasite,
I live off the cold corpus of fine print,
Habited with black robes and heart of flint,
The word made flesh for me and me alone.
I gnaw and gnaw the satisfactory bone.

DEATH AS A MEMBER OF
THE HAARLEM GUILD OF ST. LUKE

Not just another Hals, all starch and ruff—
Some boorish member of the bourgeoisie—
I am an artisan; take note of me:
Cabinetmaker, *intarsiatori* buff,
With a honed scalpel delicate enough
To limn foreshortened lutes, books, masonry
In pearwood, sandalwood and ebony,
As a marquetry still life, a *trompe l'oeil* bluff.
And yet my clients, scorning expertise,
As if my carving hand were called in doubt,
Venture capriciously to do without
Even lapped, fished, or mitered joints, decline
My chiseled skills, discountenance my fees
And settle for a simple box of pine.

DEATH THE KNIGHT

I am my lady's champion, a knight *sans peur,*
Though bitterly reproached by everyone.
She is the world's night nurse and *paix du coeur,*
Faithful and chaste as a dark-habited nun.

When in my armor I am coldly dressed,
My noble lady's favor you may see
Boldly displayed upon my helmet's crest.
Defer to her: *La Belle Dame Sans Merci.*

DEATH THE ARCHBISHOP

*. . . and the almond tree shall flourish, and the
grasshopper shall be a burden, and desire shall
fail; because man goeth to his long home; and
the mourners go about the streets.*

Ah my poor erring flock,
Truant and slow to come unto my ways,
    Making an airy mock
Of those choice pastures where my chosen graze,
You loiter childishly in pleasure's maze,
    Unheedful of the clock.

Mere tuneless vanities
Deflect you from the music of my word;
    You haste or take your ease
As if your cadences could be deferred,
Giving your whole consent to brief, absurd
    And piping symphonies.

The crozier, alb and cope
Compose the ancient blazons of my truth
    Whose broad intent and scope
Shows how discordant are the glees of youth,
How weak the serum of that serpent's tooth
    The ignorant call *Hope.*

Yet shall you come to see
In articles and emblems of my faith
    That in mortality
Lies all our comfort, as the preacher saith,
And to the blessèd kingdom of the wraith
    I have been given the key.

DEATH THE SOCIETY LADY

*Now get you to my lady's chamber, and tell
her, let her paint an inch thick, to this
favor she must come; let her laugh at that.*

Money, my dear, is my Demosthenes,
Gilead's balm, Lord God of maître d's,
Granting, like innocence, untroubled sleep,
While ugliness is no more than skin-deep.

DEATH THE POET

A BALLADE-LAMENT FOR THE MAKERS

Where have they gone, the lordly makers,
Torchlight and fire-folk of our skies,
Those grand authorial earthshakers
Who brought such gladness to the eyes
Of the knowing and unworldly-wise
In damasked language long ago?
Call them and nobody replies.
Et nunc in pulvere dormio.

The softly-spoken verbal Quakers
Who made no fuss and told no lies;
Baroque and intricate risk-takers,
Full of elliptical surprise
From Mother Goose to Paradise
Lost and Regained, where did they go?
This living hand indites, and dies,
Et nunc in pulvere dormio.

Old Masters, thunderous as the breakers
Tennyson's eloquence defies,
Beneath uncultivated acres
Our great original, Shakespeare, lies
With Grub Street hacks he would despise,
Quelled by the common ratio
That cuts all scribblers down to size,
Et nunc in pulvere dormio.

Archduke of Darkness, who supplies
The deadline governing joy and woe,
Here I put off my flesh disguise
Et nunc in pulvere dormio.

DEATH THE PAINTER

Snub-nosed, bone-fingered, deft with engraving tools,
    I have alone been given
The powers of Joshua, who stayed the sun
    In its traverse of heaven.
Here in this Gotham of unnumbered fools
I have sought out and arrested everyone.

Under my watchful eye all human creatures
    Convert to a *still life,*
As with unique precision I apply
    White lead and palette knife.
A model student of remodelled features,
The final barber, the last beautician, I.

You lordlings, what is Man, his blood and vitals,
    When all is said and done?
A poor forked animal, a nest of flies.
    Tell us, what is this one
Once shorn of all his dignities and titles,
Divested of his testicles and eyes?

DEATH THE JUDGE

Here's Justice, blind as a bat,
(Blind, if you like, as Love)
And yet, because of that,
Supreme exemplar of

Unbiased inquiry,
Knowing ahead of time
That nobody is free
Of crime or would-be crime,

And in accordance (closed
To Fortitude, Repentance,
Compassion) has composed
His predetermined sentence,

And in his chambers sits
Below a funeral wreath
And grimaces and spits
And grins and picks his teeth.

DEATH THE MEXICAN
REVOLUTIONARY

Wines of the great châteaux
Have been uncorked for you;
Come, take this terrace chair;
Examine the menu.
The view from here is such
As cannot find a match,
For even as you dine
You're so placed as to watch
Starvation in our streets
That gives your canapé
A more exquisite taste
By contrast, like the play
Of shadow and of light.
The misery of the poor
Appears, as on TV,
Set off by the allure
And glamour of the ads.
We recommend the quail,
Which you'd do well to eat
Before your powers fail,
For I inaugurate
A brand-new social order
Six cold, decisive feet
South of the border.

DEATH THE PUNCHINELLO

KENT: *This is not altogether fool, my lord.*
FOOL: *No, faith, lords and great men will not let me. If I had a monopoly out, they would have part on't. And ladies too, they will not let me have all the fool to myself; they'll be snatching.*

Two servants were paid to set his house on fire
And, when he fled, to pierce him with little darts.
And so this man, widely praised and admired,

Envied by many, a soldier, philosopher,
A young Adonis, was dead at forty-six.
So much, alas, for Alcibiades.
Now as for me, admittedly grotesque,
Cheated of feature by dissembling Nature,
Bearing an envious mountain on my back
Where sits deformity to mock my body,
I'm your imperishable comedian.
I suffer multi-interments, executions,
Yet like Donne's lovers, I die and rise the same,
Vulgar, mean, selfish, undefeatable.
You wouldn't think me much to look at me,
A clown's hooked nose and all the rest of it,
Yet, for all that, I have a way with women.
Love 'em and leave 'em, as I like to say.
And nothing pleases the kids more than my cudgel.
They see the justice of it, don't you see.
How, against all odds, this ugly man,
Hated, unmanumitted just like them,
Wields his big stick and whacks authority
Hard on its wooden head. I lack the graces
That everyone observed in the young Greek,
Women and men alike. He grew so vain
He wouldn't play the flute, claimed it distorted
The sculptural virtues of his classic features.
That, I would venture to say, is not my problem.
You find me always dressed, made-up, in white,
All dredged in flour, like an apprentice baker,
Though sometimes masked, like your Jack Ketch, in black.
And you, my dears, are the butt of all my jokes.
In candor, I admit some do not like me.
They call me "Toad," and they would not be far
From the truth, if only they were speaking German.
Nevertheless, in spite of such abuse,
I have a joke that always breaks them up.
Mine's the last laugh, the terminal ha-ha.
As the poet said, *"Ce crapaud-là, c'est moi."*

DEATH THE WHORE

I

Some thin gray smoke twists up against a sky
Of German silver in the sullen dusk
From a small chimney among leafless trees.
The paths are empty, the weeds bent and dead;
Winter has taken hold. And what, my dear,
Does this remind you of? You are surprised
By the familiar manner, the easy, sure
Intimacy of my address. You wonder,
Whose curious voice is this? Why should that scene
Seem distantly familiar? Did something happen
Back in my youth on a deserted path
Late on some unremembered afternoon?
And now you'll feel at times a fretful nagging
At the back of your mind as of something almost grasped
But tauntingly and cunningly evasive.
It may go on for months, perhaps for years.
Think of the memory game that children played
So long ago. A grownup brought a tray
Laden with objects hidden by a shawl
Or coverlet with fine brocaded flowers
Beneath which, like the roofs of a small city,
Some secret things lay cloaked. Then at a signal
The cloth was whisked away for thirty seconds.
You were allowed to do nothing but look,
And then the cover was replaced. Remember?
The tray contained bright densely crowded objects,
Sometimes exotic—a small cloisonné egg,
A candle-snuffer with an ivory handle—
But simple things as well. It never occurred
To any of the children there to count them;
You had been told simply to memorize
The contents of the tray. Each child was given

Paper and pencil to list what he recalled
And no one ever finally got them all;
Something always escaped. Perhaps a needle,
A gum eraser or a plastic ruler.
And so it is that now, as you're about
To eat or light a cigarette, something
Passes too swiftly before you can take aim,
Passes in furtive silence, in disguise,
Glimpsed only hazily in retrospect—
Like a clock's strokes recounted once they're done,
Never with confidence.

                   And now you're angry
At what you think of as my long digression
When in fact it's the eclipses of your mind,
Those sink-holes, culverts, cisterns long avoided
As dangerous, where the actual answer lies.
As for my indirection, I'll just say
I have more time than I know what to do with.
Let me give you a hint. The voice you hear
Is not the voice of someone you remember—
Or rather, it's that voice now greatly altered
By certain events of which you've partly heard,
Partly imagined, altogether feared.
Does that help? No, I didn't think it would.
Perhaps we can return another time
(A time when you're conveniently abstracted)
To the topic of my voice and of that smoke.

I I

Much time elapses. (I could count the days;
You, for your part, have no idea how many.)
Today a color ad for undergarments,
Some glossy pages of *Victoria's Secret*,
Modeled by a young blonde catches your eye.
Nothing so vivid as a memory

Results. Perhaps a vague erotic sense,
A fleeting impulse down between your legs,
Stirs like a sleeping dog. Your mind begins
Its little, paltry Leporello's list
Of former girlfriends who pass in review
As images, stripped even of their names.
And then you linger upon one. It's me.
Don't be surprised. All that was long ago.
Your indolent thought goes over my young breasts,
Remembering, fondling, exciting you.
How very long ago that was. It lasted
Almost two years. Two mainly happy years.
In all that time, what did you learn of me?
My name, my body, how best to go about
Mutual arousal, my taste in food and drink
And what would later be called "substances."
(These days among my friends I might be called
"A woman of substance" if I were still around.)
You also learned, from a casual admission,
That I had twice attempted suicide.
Tact on both sides had left this unexplored.
We both seemed to like sex for the same reason.
It was, as they used to say, a "little death,"
A tiny interval devoid of thought
When even sensation is so localized
Only one part of the body seems alive.
And when you left I began the downhill slope.
First one-night stands; then quickly I turned pro
In order to get all the drugs I wanted.
My looks went fast. I didn't really care.
The thing that I'd been after from the first,
With you, with sex, with drugs, was oblivion.
So it was easy. A simple overdose
Knocked back with half a bottle of good Scotch.
In later years the rumors found you out
Through mutual friends. And somehow you remembered
That I had been disowned by my family.

My parents would have nothing to do with me
After they found I'd been a prostitute,
To say nothing of my trial suicides.
So, as you guessed, when I at last succeeded,
They acted as if I never had been born.
("Let the day perish . . . ," as the scripture says.)
There was no funeral, no cemetery,
Nowhere for you to come in pilgrimage—
Although from time to time you thought of me.
Oh yes, my dear, you thought of me; I know.
But less and less, of course, as time went on.
And then you learned by a chance word of mouth
That I had been cremated, thereby finding
More of oblivion than I'd even hoped for.
And now when I occur to you, the voice
You hear is not the voice of what I was
When young and sexy and perhaps in love,
But the weary voice shaped in your later mind
By a small sediment of fact and rumor,
A faceless voice, a voice without a body.

As for the winter scene of which I spoke—
The smoke, my dear, the smoke. I am the smoke.

DEATH THE FILM DIRECTOR

Open with a long shot. Chimneys and spires
Of the old town, rouged in the copper glow
Of sunset. Intense, arterial red
Dyeing the trees as day slowly expires,
Staining the churches, pathways, fence-posts, spread
From roof to roof, while, rising from below,
Cool tides of shadow lap the countryside,
Engulf the cemetery headstones, shroud
Arbor, toolshed, curbstone and portico.
Now from behind a lazily drifting cloud
A full, Pierrot-white moon; its bleaching light
Drains the lifeblood of everything in sight.
Zoom down to a derelict alley, a scrawny cat
Sniffing through toppled garbage till it finds
A male, black-skinned, mature, immobile hand,
Its parent limb, head, body, all concealed
By liquor cartons, broken Venetian blinds,
Worn tires, an unravelled welcome mat.
The creature paws at a finger, which remains
Inert, sniffs once again, looks up and walks
Calmly across the hand into the dark.
Credits. The title, the studio, the stars
Flash on, then fade. Henry Mancini noise.
And then my name glows on the darkened screen.
It lingers there a while, etching the mind
Of every member of the audience.
As well it should. This film required of me
Immense executive abilities—
All those subordinates to keep in line,
Trained to alert me with their signal cries:
"Ready when *you* are, C.B." That's what I like,
That fine docility. As for the cast,
If the truth be known, actors are idiots.
Theirs is the glamour, of course. Their gorgeous looks,

Along with large, unmerited salaries,
Must compensate them for their tiny minds.
But in the end, after repeated takes,
The prints, the cutting-room floor, I am the one
Who sees that everything falls into place,
The master plan. This film has a large cast,
A huge cast; countless, you might almost say;
And for them all, for every one of them,
I have designed, with supreme artfulness,
What could be called an inevitable plot.

DEATH THE COPPERPLATE PRINTER

I turn Christ's cross till it turns Catherine's wheel,
Ixion's wheel becoming Andrew's cross,
    All four being windlass ways
To press my truth full home, force you to feel
    The brevity of your days,
Your strength's, health's, teeth's, desire's and memory's loss.

The bitten plate, removed from its Dutch Bath
Of mordants, has been set below a screw
    That will enforce my will
Like the press that crushed Isaiah's grapes of wrath.
    My lightest touch can kill,
My costly first impressions can subdue.

Slowly I crank my winch, and the bones crack,
The skull splits open and the ribs give way.
    Who, then, thinks to endure?
Confess the artistry of my attack;
    Admire the fine gravure,
The trenched darks, the cross-hatching, the pale gray.

This is no metaphor. Margaret Clitherow,
A pious woman, even as she prayed
    Was cheated of her breath
By a court verdict that some years ago
    Ordered her pressed to death.
I'm always grateful for such human aid.

DEATH THE SCHOLAR

No opinion, however absurd or incredible, can be imagined which has not been maintained by one of the philosophers. DESCARTES

I bide my time, you see, I bide my time.
Recently I resumed work on the classics.
I find among these well-patinaed relics
Some glacier-capped *aiguilles* of the sublime.

Sophocles, for example: *The best of fates . . .*
And the Elder Pliny: *The supreme happiness
Of life is that it end abruptly.* Yes,
We share these quiet, twin-skulled *tête-a-têtes.*

Come, let me be the tutor to your hopes.
My scholarly emendations can expose
All your most cherished errors. I am of those
Who may be called authentic philanthropes.

Ignorance: the one unpardonable crime.
Your Solons, Stagirites, your *philosophes*
To me are countrified, unpolished oafs.
I bide my time, you see, I bide my time.

DEATH THE CARNIVAL BARKER

con brio

Step forward, please! Make room for those in back!
Come in and see the greatest show on earth!
I promise it will take your breath away!
Something you're sure to call your money's worth;
And bound to last forever and a day!
Softer than down; more powerful than crack!

Flame-eaters, jugglers, the two-headed boy
Are merely trifles by comparison.
We've got the ultimate show to freak you out.
The surest cure for worry under the sun—
As well as toothache, blindness, debt and gout.
There's nothing that you'll ever more enjoy!

The little lady with the long blonde hair
Will issue you a ticket for the price
Of your life savings, your miserable estate,
The shirt right off your back. Take my advice:
It's the best deal you'll ever get. Why wait?
We're known throughout the world as fair and square.

And talk of fairness! Talk of equality!
Give me your poor, your homeless. I admit
The halt, the deaf, all races and all trades.
O you rejected ones, unwashed, unfit,
Entrust yourselves to the keeping of my aids.
No quota, bribe, initiation fee!

No one has ever asked for his money back!
Geniuses, beauties, all the greatest wits
Have been our patrons! Once the show's begun
Small kids admitted for a mere two-bits!
Fear not, my friends! There's room for everyone!
Step forward, please! Make room for those in back!

49

I I PROUST ON SKATES

THE WHIRLIGIG OF TIME

HORACE I:25

They are fewer these days, those supple, suntanned boys
Whose pebbles tapped at your window, and your door
Swings less and less on its obliging hinges
For wildly importunate suitors. Fewer the cries
Of "Lydia, how can you sleep when I've got the hots?
I won't last out the night; let me get my rocks off."
Things have moved right along, and, behold, it's you
Who quails, like a shriveled whore, as they scorn and
    dodge you,
And the wind shrieks like a sex-starved thing in heat
As the moon goes dark and the mouth of your old dry
    vulva
Rages and hungers, and your worst, most ulcerous pain
Is knowing those sleek-limbed boys prefer the myrtle,
The darling buds of May, leaving dried leaves
To cluster in unswept corners, fouling doorways.

A RUMINANT

As Sir Osbert Sitwell has remarked,
human beings display "the identical
combination of flaming pride and meek
submission that in the animal world
distinguishes the camel."

MARTIN C. D'ARCY, S.J.
The Mind and Heart of Love

Out of the Urdu, into our instant ken,
ambles the gross molester of the Sphinx,
    our *oont,* or camel,
hunchbacked from failed exertions, poor Ur-Punch
and brigand-clown of Noah's passengers,
    the Hebrew *gimel*

for the deformity it's luck to touch.
Footpadded and austere, a temperance leader,
    he slumps in torpid
reverie over a sea of blistering dunes,
yet easily is tamed, the Britannica says,
    because he's stupid.

Beware his soulful glances that conceal
absence of thought and the ferocity
    of a seasoned bigot,
who nevertheless briefly became the bearer
of kings and spices, the royal pattern of patience,
    and wisdom's legate.

PROSPECTS

We have set out from here for the sublime
Pastures of summer shade and mountain stream;
I have no doubt we shall arrive on time.

Is all the green of that enameled prime
A snapshot recollection or a dream?
We have set out from here for the sublime

Without provisions, without one thin dime,
And yet, for all our clumsiness, I deem
It certain that we shall arrive on time.

No guidebook tells you if you'll have to climb
Or swim. However foolish we may seem,
We have set out from here for the sublime

And must get past the scene of an old crime
Before we falter and run out of steam,
Riddled by doubt that we'll arrive on time.

Yet even in winter a pale paradigm
Of birdsong utters its obsessive theme.
We have set out from here for the sublime;
I have no doubt we shall arrive on time.

FOR JAMES MERRILL: AN ADIEU

As fadeth Sommers-sunne from gliding fountaines

The daily press keeps up-to-date obits
Cooling in morgues and is piously prepared
For the claim that any day may be one's last.
Dictators, famous short-stops, felons, wits
Intimately recline in darkly shared
Beds of fine print, their leaden, predestined past.

But you, dear friend, managed to slip away,
Actually disappear in the dead of winter
More perfectly than Yeats. As at a show,
While we were savoring all your skills, the play
Of your words, your elegant, serious banter,
You cloaked yourself, vanished like Prospero

Or Houdini, escaping from cold padlocked fact,
Manacles, blindfolds, all our earthly ties,
And there we sat, the master illusionist
Leaving us stunned in the middle of his act,
The stage vacant, expecting some surprise
Reentry from the wings to a rousing Liszt

Fanfare, tumultuous applause, a bow
And a gentle, pleased, self-deprecating smile.
There comes no manager hither to explain.
Words fail us, from the weak and fatuous "ciao,
Bello," to the bellowing grand style,
As we shuffle out to the shabby street and the rain.

You are now one of that chosen band and choice
Fellowship gathered at Sandover's sunlit end,
Fit audience though few, where, at their ease,
Dante, Rilke, Mallarmé, Proust rejoice
In the rich polyphony of their latest friend,
Scored in his sweetly noted higher keys.

SISTERS

How like a golden floating benediction
The morning sunlight loiters among leaves,
Emblazons tossing billows of gnats, unhives
Its honeyed treasure, and confers election

Upon all souls, on every blessed one
Here in this compound proctored by St. Vincent
De Paul in marble patience, and with ambient
Warmth anoints each blossom, twig and stone,

And the poor, baffled patients, shy as gerbils,
Hemmed in like helpless pets. They wander here
Over clipped lawns and through delicious air
In a second childhood, having lost their marbles.

One of them writes home to her elder brother,
"We had a birthday out in the violent ward.
I won a prize. The craziest can't play cards.
It's all they can do to converse about the weather.

Wouldn't you buy me a small graphaphone?
It wouldn't cost more than ten or twenty dollars,
Would it? A few old discs might serve as healers:
Stardust, perhaps, *Deep Purple*, *All My Own*.

We could dance to them and have some pleasant times.
It's allowed, I think. And the sisters wouldn't mind
If the music wasn't church but some good band.
(I'd want the smallest graphaphone that comes.)"

And the youngest nurses, made beautiful with care,
Sisters of Charity, escort the feeble
Through inward terrors, through memories that disable,
From dark brown hallways out into morning air,

To agate swirls and citrines of the sun,
Sparrows at their dust-baths, shameless, surprising
These scrubbed, diligent girls, their starched coifs rising
Like spinnakers, flame-white tongues of cyclamen.

THE MESSAGE

Fuscus, my friend, go tell that lying . . . Wait!
Hold on a moment. Let me reformulate
The sort of thing I'm after. Tell her she,
Whether she likes the thought or not, will be . . .
Or, rather, let me put it another way.
Say that you left me reveling, and say
Everyone says how good-natured I am.
And let her know I'm happy as a clam.

THE MYSTERIES OF CAESAR

Known to the boys in his Latin class as "Sir,"
Balding, cologned, mild-mannered Mr. Sypher
Defied his sentence as a highschool lifer
With a fresh, carefully chosen boutonniere

As daily he heard the Helvetians plead their cause
In chains while captives were brought face to face
With the impositions of the ablative case,
The torts and tortures of grammatic laws.

Gracelessly stalled by vast impediments
Of words and baggage as by a conqueror's shackles,
O'Rourke, his face a celestial sphere of freckles
(One Gaul brought down by the pluperfect tense)

Submitted to all the galls and agonies
Of pained sight-readings from the *Gallic Wars.*
They all bore dark, dishonorable scars
From what their textbook called an "exercise"

At least as draining as the quarter-mile.
But Mr. Sypher listened with superb
Imperial hauteur, with imperturb-
able patience, and a somewhat cryptic smile.

"Thompson," he'd murmur, "please instruct our class."
And Thompson would venture, timidly, much rattled,
"Caesar did withhold his men from battle,
And he did have enough in presentness

To prohibit the enemy from further wastings,
From foragings and rapines." And through a long
Winter campaign of floundering, grief, and wrong,
That little army force-marched without resting.

"Please aid us, Jones," Mr. Sypher would beseech;
And Jones would tremulously undertake
To decipher the old Caesarian mystique
In the mixed medium of cracked parts of speech.

"Which things being known, when surest things accede,
He did deem enough of cause ... ," Jones volunteered.
Invariably it came out sounding weird,
The garbled utterance of some lesser breed

Without the law of common intercourse.
Long weeks of rain, followed by early frost
Had not improved morale, and yet the worst
Is not when there can always still be worse.

They rather liked Mr. Sypher, who was kind,
An easy grader. Was he a widower?
It was thought he had lost a child some years before.
Often they wondered what passed through his mind

As he calmly attended to their halt and crude
Efforts, not guessing one or another boy
Served as Antinous to that inward eye
Which is the pitiless bliss of solitude.

TO FORTUNA PARVULORUM

*Young men have strong passions, and tend
to gratify them indiscriminately . . . they
show absence of self-control . . . they are hot
tempered. Their lives are mainly spent not
in memory but in expectation . . . The
character of Elderly Men [is different]. They
have lived many years; they have often been
taken in, and often made mistakes; and life
on the whole is a bad business.*

ARISTOTLE, *Rhetoric*, II, 12.

As a young man I was headstrong, willful, rash,
    Determined to amaze,
Grandly indifferent to comfort as to cash,
Past Envy's sneer, past Age's toothless gnash,
    Boldly I went my ways.

Then I matured. I sacrificed the years
    Lost in impetuous folly
To calm Prudentia, paying my arrears
For heedlessness in the cautious coin of fears
    And studious melancholy.

Now, having passed the obligatory stations,
    I turn in turn to you,
Divinity of diminished expectations,
To whom I direct these tardy supplications,
    Having been taught how few

Are blessed enough to encounter on their way
    The least chipped glint of joy,
And learned in what altered tones I hear today
The remembered words, *"Messieurs, les jeux sont faits,"*
    That stirred me as a boy.

A PLEDGE

Beauty of face, of body, and of spirit
Join with such grace in her of whom I write
No dreams of man or woman might come near it;
Yet she is wed, in heaven or hell's despite,
To an ignoble, titled troglodyte
For whom our pitiful language has no words
Sufficiently uncouth and impolite.
The air is sweetest that a thistle guards.

He'd have that lady's mind-inspiring merit
Kept secret, all her virtues out of sight,
Imprisoned in his castle's tallest turret,
His bushel basket stifling all her light,
Insensible of inwit's agenbite.
She who deserves the homages of bards
Languishes a neglected Shulamite.
The air is sweetest that a thistle guards.

But her great worth, beyond the count of karat,
Shall not be his alone if appetite,
Wit and determination may secure it.
Devotion such as mine must claim its right.
Gaul, like the afterlife, is tripartite,
And this ménage will shake down into thirds.
Odors of myrrh and nard invade the night.
The air is sweetest that a thistle guards.

Duke, you are unaware of your true plight;
Antlers and scorn for you are in the cards.
I have a yearning she shall yet requite:
The air is sweetest that a thistle guards.

THE LIFE OF CRIME

Burdened from birth with a lean Methodist
Father in daily touch with the Sublime,
It was small wonder I should turn to crime
As, of all methods to survive, the best.

Had I not often witnessed how a few
Spasmodic yeas and epigastric glories
Delivered inveterate sinners of all their worries,
Transported hopeless scoundrels from the pew

Of sin to the very otto of sanctity?
How refreshing it was, this early morning dip
In the Blood of the Lamb–how tempting to swim a lap,
Then shower and change before the *réchauffé*

Of habitual vice. Still, at an early age
I implored my father to be permitted to see
Kinkaid's New Travelling Menagerie,
Dreamed of as the Arabian cortège

That accompanied Melchior and Balthazar
To the crib from exotic ziggurat pavilions.
This was the era before my great rebellion,
When father and son had hopes for one another.

And then the day came. I could actually tell,
Before seeing the cages, flags, and tents,
The presence of those lithe inhabitants
Of Ali Baba's kingdom by their smell:

A strong sexual musk, filling the lung
With heated bestial vigor. Bales of straw
Scattered beneath the strut of hoof and paw
Mingled their scent with the raw odor of dung

As an incontestable presence and true sign
Of the animals I was about to see.
But as we entered, father lectured me
On the real nature of this nomadic shrine.

The camel was God's symbol for the grace
Of patience, never mind his sorrowful eyes;
The lion God's assurance we shall rise
Like Gospeler Mark from this polluted place.

And so to him the panther, the baboon,
Giraffe and walrus all were allegories,
Dim shapes enacting hobbled moral stories,
Denied even their smells that all too soon

Thinned and departed, like the Christmas kings,
Their turbans fine as smoke, their lives a tale
Told to instruct a child. The world, turned pale,
Exposed an absence at the core of things.

It was not long before I found I loathed
The pastor and his self-absolving flock,
And prided myself when I had learned to pick
The pockets of all the elegantly clothed.

LÀ-BAS: A TRANCE

From silk route Samarkand, emeralds and drugs
Find their way west, smuggled by leather-capped
Bandits with lard-greased hair across unmapped
Storm-tossed sand oceans drained to the very dregs,

And thence to such ports of call as Amsterdam,
The waters of its intricate canals
Gold-leafed and amethyst-shadowed by the veils
Of cloud-occluded suns, imaged in dim

Hempen mirages and opium reveries
Crowding the mind of a Parisian poet
With jasmine adornments to his barren garret,
The masts of frigates from all seven seas

Moored just outside his window, their bright rigging
What all his neighbors know as laundry lines.
France is as nothing; France and her finest wines
For all this fellow's interest can go begging

As the doors of his perception open wide
Admitting nothing but those nacreous errors
Harvested from unfathomed depths of mirrors:
Harems of young, voluptuous, sloe-eyed

Houris, undressed, awaiting his commands,
Untiring courtyard fountains casting jewels
Thriftlessly into blue-and-white-tiled pools,
Their splashes mingled with languid sarabandes.

Carpaccio's Middle East evokes an air-borne
Carpet, a sash and headgear the color of flame
Turned into Holland's tulips whose very name
Comes to him from the Turkish word for turban.

MATISSE: BLUE INTERIOR WITH TWO GIRLS–1947

*. . . he lived through some of the most
traumatic political events of recorded
history, the worst wars, the greatest
slaughters, the most demented rivalries of
ideology, without, it seems, turning a
hair. . . . Perhaps Matisse did suffer from
fear and loathing like the rest of us, but
there is no trace of them in his work. His
studio was a world within a world: a place
of equilibrium that, for sixty continuous
years, produced images of comfort, refuge,
and balanced satisfaction.*

ROBERT HUGHES, *The Shock of the New*

Outside is variable May, a lawn of immediate green,
   The tree as blue as its shadow.
      A shutter angles out in charitable shade.
It is a world of yearning: we yearn for it,
   Its youthful natives yearn for one another.
      Their flesh is firm as a plum, their smooth tanned waists,
Lit through the fluttered leaves above their heads,
   Are rubbed and cinctured with this morning's bangles.
      Yet each, if we but take thought, is a lean gnomon,
A bone finger with its moral point:
   The hour, the minute, the dissolving pleasure.
      (Light fails, the shadows pool themselves in hollows.)
Here, in the stifling fragrance of mock orange,
   In the casual glance, the bright lust of the eye,
      Lies the hot spring of inevitable tears.

Within is the cool blue perfect cube of thought.
   The branched spirea carefully arranged
      Is no longer random growth: it now becomes
The object of our thought, it becomes our thought.
   The room is a retreat in which the drone
      Of the electric fan is modest, unassertive,

Faithful, as with a promise of lemonade
    And other gentle solaces of summer,
        Among which, for the two serene young girls
In this cool tank of blue is an open book
    Where they behold the pure unchanging text
        Of manifold, reverberating depth,
Quiet and tearless in its permanence.
    Deep in their contemplation the two girls,
        Regarding art, have become art themselves.
Once out of nature, they have settled here
    In this blue room of thought, beyond the reach
        Of the small brief sad ambitions of the flesh.

PROUST ON SKATES

*He stayed in bed, and at the beginning of
October still wasn't getting up till two in
the afternoon. But he made a seventy mile
journey to Chamonix to join Albu* [Louis
Albufera] *and Louisa* [de Mornand,
Albufera's beautiful mistress] *on a
mule-back excursion to Montanvert, where
they went skating.*

RONALD HAYMAN
Proust: A Biography

The alpine forests, like huddled throngs of mourners,
Black, hooded, silent, resign themselves to wait
    As long as may be required;
A low pneumonia mist covers the glaciers,
Spruces are bathed in a cold sweat, the late
    Sun has long since expired,

Though barely risen, and the gray cast of the day
Is stark, unsentimental, and metallic.
    Earth-stained and chimney-soiled
Snow upon path and post is here to stay,
Foundered in endless twilight, a poor relic
    Of a once gladder world.

Sparse café patrons can observe a few
Skaters skimming the polished soapstone lake,
    A platform for their skill
At crosscut, grapevine, loop and curlicue,
Engelmann's Star, embroideries that partake
    Of talent, coaching, drill,

While a few tandem lovers, hand in hand,
Perform their *pas de deux* along the edges,
    Oblivious, unconcerned.
This is a stony, vapor-haunted land
Of granite dusk, of wind sieved by the hedges,
    Their branches braced and thorned.

Escaped from the city's politics and fribble,
Hither has come an odd party of three,
    Braided by silken ties:
With holiday abandon, the young couple
Have retreated into the deep privacy
    Of one another's eyes,

While the third, who in different ways yet loves them both,
Finds himself now, as usual, all alone,
    And lacing on his skates,
Steadies himself, cautiously issues forth
Into the midst of strangers and his own
    Interior debates.

Sweatered and mufflered to protect the weak
And lacey branches of his bronchial tree
    From the fine-particled threat
Of the moist air, he curves in an oblique
And gentle gradient, floating swift and free —
    No *danseur noble,* and yet

He glides with a gaining confidence, inscribes
Tentative passages, thinks again, backtracks,
    Comes to a minute point,
Then wheels about in widening sweeps and lobes,
Large Palmer cursives and smooth *entrelacs,*
    Preoccupied, intent

On a subtle, long-drawn style and pliant script
Incised with twin steel blades and qualified
    Perfectly to express,
With arms flung wide or gloved hands firmly gripped
Behind his back, attentively, clear-eyed,
    A glancing happiness.

It will not last, that happiness; nothing lasts;
But will reduce in time to the clear brew
    Of simmering memory
Nourished by shadowy gardens, music, guests,
Childhood affections, and, of Delft, a view
    Steeped in a sip of tea.

A DEATH IN WINTER

In memory of Joseph Brodsky,
born May 24, 1940, Leningrad;
died January 28, 1996, Brooklyn

Delicate sensors registered the shock,
Cool scanners shuddered but went unobserved;
It was very dark, of course, the city scarved
In the sleeping death of each day's life, each clock

Reckoning that brief moment only in passing.
Historian, watchman, made their careful note
Of power surges and ebbs, who's in, who's out.
At the hourly Bellevue bed-check no one was missing.

But this tremor, beyond the ten-tone Richter scale,
Unsettles us more, with its quiet ultra-sound,
Than cold tectonic plates, the underground
Turning of coats and strata, the old turmoil

And trepidation of societies and spheres.
Spaces are mourners. Prospect Park is the first
To cloak itself in darkness. Well rehearsed,
The Nevsky Prospect blacks out, disappears,

And before St. Mark's, the whole world's living room
Empties and floats away (as the spirit does)
With its pigeons and its tiny orchestras,
While the Luxembourg's stone gentry pace and roam

In solitary grief. Time itself mourns,
Going back to the same hour as if in search,
Time and again, of bedroom, study, porch,
In nightly, demented, desperate returns,

Looking for something lost, a loss untold,
Greater than many of us understand.
In the Republic of Letters one fine hand,
Cyrillic, cursive, American, has been stilled.

Survivor of show trial, of state oppression,
Exiled from parents, language, neighborhood,
This man's was the lasting sovereignty of the word,
Beyond the grasp of politics or fashion,

The hawk's domain and climate, whose largesse
Comes as a gift of snow from the obscure
Mid-winter gray in verse precise and pure.
He now dwells in the care of each of us.

Reader, dwell with his poems. Underneath
Their gaiety and music, note the chilled strain
Of irony, of felt and mastered pain,
The sound of someone laughing through clenched teeth.

NOTES

DEATH THE HYPOCRITE: "Some bristlecone pines are the oldest living things on earth. . . . a total of seventeen bristlecone pines have been found which, still living and growing, are over 4,000 years old, the oldest some 4,600 years old." Andreas Feininger, *Trees.*

DEATH THE POET: *Et nunc in pulvere dormio* (And now I sleep in the dust) is appropriated from a refrain in John Skelton's "Lament For the Death of the Noble Prince Edward the Fourth," which, in turn, was borrowed from an anonymous Middle English lyric that begins, "I hadde richesse, I hadde my helthe. . . ."

DEATH THE PUNCHINELLO: Some lines of Shakespeare's Richard of Gloucester (from *Henry VI*) have been appropriated, as has the last line, taken from Tristan Corbière's "*Le Crapaud.*"

DEATH THE COPPERPLATE PRINTER: Metaphors in the opening stanzas are borrowed from emblems, some of them identified by Rosemond Tuve in *A Reading of George Herbert,* where she writes of "the use of a set of conceits clustered around the ancient symbol of Christ as the miraculous grape-bunch," and remarks that this is "closely connected with various other symbols and conceits: Christ in the wine-press of the Cross . . ." Jacob Cornelisz. van Oostsanen's brown ink drawing, *Allegory of the Sacrifice of the Mass* (*The Age of Bruegel,* National Gallery of Art) employs the same conceit in visual form. "Dutch Bath" is the name of a mordant used in copperplate etching; it is composed of dilute hydrochloric acid mixed with chlorate of potash. Saint Margaret Clitherow (1556–1586), a devout Roman Catholic convert from the Anglican Church, was pressed to death with an 800-pound weight for harboring Catholic clergy.

DEATH THE SCHOLAR: Stagirite=Aristotle

THE MESSAGE: Adapted from a poem by Meleager in the Greek Anthology.

THE MYSTERIES OF CAESAR: Antinous was the favorite of the emperor Hadrian, by whose command statues of the young man, after his death, were set up in major cities throughout the empire.

THE LIFE OF CRIME: The poem was prompted by a passage in Mayhew's *London Labour and the London Poor.*

PROUST ON SKATES: Engelmann's Star is an elaborate pattern for figure skating, devised by one E. Engelmann, the Austrian skating champion of Europe in 1894. The "view of Delft" is a Vermeer painting that deeply impressed and affected Proust when he saw it in the Mauritshuis at The Hague in 1902.

A DEATH IN WINTER: Sleep as "the death of each day's life," *Macbeth,* II, ii; "who's in, who's out," *King Lear,* V, ii; "trepidation of the spheres," John Donne, "A Valediction Forbidding Mourning"; Henry James referred to the Piazza San Marco as "a great drawing room, the drawing room of Europe"; statuary in the Luxembourg Gardens figures in Brodsky's poem-sequence "Twenty Sonnets to Mary Queen of Scots"; the hawk and snow are borrowed from Brodsky's poem "The Hawk's Cry in Autumn"; the "sensors" and "scanners" at the beginning owe something to the "instruments" in the opening of Auden's poem "In Memory of William Butler Yeats," just as "the sovereignty of the word" is indebted to Auden's homage to "language" in the same poem.

A NOTE ON THE TYPE

The text of this book was set in a typeface called Walbaum, named for Justus Erich Walbaum (1768–1839), a typefounder who removed from his beginnings in Goslar to Weimar in 1803. It is likely that he produced this famous typeface shortly thereafter, following the designs of the French typefounder, Firmin Didot. His original matrices are still in existence, owned by the Berthold foundry of Berlin. Continuously popular in Germany since its inception, the face was introduced to England by the Monotype Corporation in 1934, and has steadily grown in popularity ever since.

Composition by Graphic Composition, Inc., Athens, Georgia
Printed and bound by Quebecor, Kingsport, Tennessee
Designed by Harry Ford